A different perpective on growing

knowledge

UNLOCKING THE KNOWLEDGE VAULT

PETER GREGERSEN

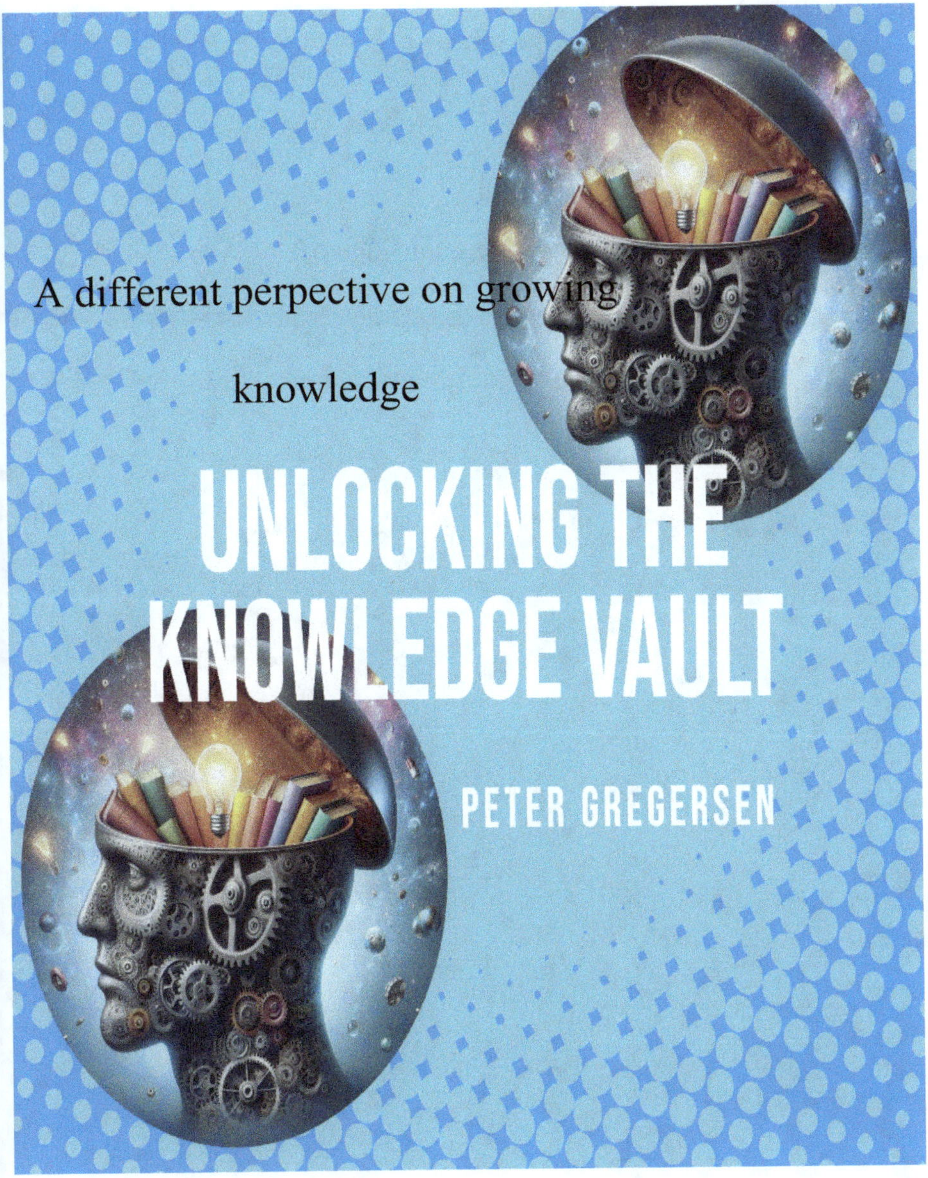

Dr Peter Gregersen © 2024

For Cheryl my patient darling wife.

Dr Peter Gregersen © 2024

Transference of knowledge

ABSTRACT

The transference of knowledge and the creation of a knowledge vault within operations of the Business sector is the cornerstone to the success of this dynamic contributor to the economy, not only as a skills developer, but also as a collective group of experts that unknowingly build a community of expertise that transfer knowledge amongst themselves within an organisation.

Dr Peter Gregersen © 2024

Leadership that share knowledge, whether tacit or implied, leads to the development and knowledge growth from members to those who are exposed to the intricacies of decision making and business practices. This leads then to the skills development and retention of the participants who feel nurtured and fulfilled in the employment within the organisation and view themselves as valued members.

There is a correlation between knowledge sharing and the desire for job security that leads to the feeling of being nurtured and finding the employment positive and enjoyable.

The transference of knowledge allows the receiver of the knowledge to develop to where the point of the receiver becoming an expert in their chosen field is attained and the collective of the mangers are developed to the level of a community of experts in their various fields.

However, the academic qualifications of leadership are low, the significance of this highlights the level of networking amongst themselves as paramount to the success of this multi- billion-rand economy.

BY

Dr Peter Gregersen

6300 words

Dr Peter Gregersen © 2024

Author

Dr Peter Gregersen

DBA, MBA

East London

capcsame@gmail.com

isbn 9798333881984

Dr Peter Gregersen © 2024

INTRODUCTION

Private businesses operate in an insular environment. However, all businesses require a return to shareholders, staff and customers. Often the shareholder and customer returns are taken care of whilst not enabling the transfer of knowledge to staff. The outcome of which is poor staff retention.

The weaknesses of a private business are that they operate in an insular fashion often controlled by a General Manager, whom being responsible for the entire operations of the business, makes all the decisions. By making all the decisions the transfer of knowledge and the creation of knowledge sharing environment does not exist leading to a dichotomous relationship between managers with attrition being inevitable.

The importance of solving this problem is to firstly reduce attrition of staff and in particular management staff and secondly to provide a framework of the transferring of knowledge, enriching and empowering middle management.

As natural attrition takes place and senior managers depart from the industry for various reason, the following question arises. Are middle managers being developed to be leaders? Are leaders progressive enough to allow this to happen or are they hindering the process?

As transformation in the workplace becomes an increased driver of change that is required in a South African context, the notion of training managers to become effective leaders bears weight that needs to be explored. The benefit of this will be realized in a reduction of staff turnover and a motivated engaged knowledgeable workforce. The obvious opportunity is the creation of a community of experts in the middle management sector creating a competitive advantage over competitors. A framework for this transferring of knowledge to create a knowledge bank needs to be designed.

BACKGROUND

Management fears of future employment and job security are very real and for these reasons managers often become problem solvers themselves. This however need not be the case if managers become enriching progressive leaders and develop people around them; the result will be felt on an increase in return to shareholders, return to customer satisfaction improvement and a motivated workforce.

Either people lead to inspire and build capable teams, "multipliers" that utilize the hidden dormant intelligence within individuals or leaders, or they sap the very essence out of people around them akin to a micro manager, "diminishers". Further stresses that companies regularly put pressure on growing revenue whilst quality deteriorates as expenses are curtailed instead of unleashing the dormant intelligence. This is explained in the following. At the core,

Dr Peter Gregersen © 2024

Multipliers and Diminishers operate from a very different set of assumptions."

Multipliers and Diminishers

: Multiplier Descriptors: "People are smart and will figure this out."		Diminisher Descriptors: "They will never figure this out Without me."	
Talent Magnet	Attracts talented people and uses them at their highest point of contribution	Empire Builder	Hoards resources and underutilizes talent
Liberator	Creates an intense environment that requires people's best thinking and work	Tyrant	Creates a tense environment that suppresses people's thinking and capability
Challenger	Defines an opportunity that causes people to stretch	Know-It-All	Gives directives that showcase how much they know
Debate Maker	Drives sound decisions through rigorous debate	Decision Maker	Makes centralized, abrupt decisions that confuse the organisation
Investor	Gives other people the ownership for results and invests in their success	Micro-Manager	Drives results through personal involvement "

Wiseman, (2011)

Dr Peter Gregersen © 2024

In support of this every company whether small or large requires a transfer of knowledge, by enthusiastically transferring knowledge between managers improves functionality. Further to this examine the culture of the relationship between the giver and the recipient of knowledge sharing as one of being based on trust, the willingness of receiving knowledge, of dispensing of knowledge and further to this a competitive advantage will be achieved in an environment conducive to knowledge sharing. The explanation of knowledge was first discussed by Plato as being the "justified true belief" or the "grasping of an idea".

Dr Peter Gregersen © 2024

Research into knowledge sharing and barriers to knowledge have revealed poor solutions to creating an environment that is conducive to improving leadership in a knowledge environment. This is further explained that these barriers are themselves seen to be viewed as a lack of knowledge largely giving little hope to individual development as various frames of references and memories do not exist.

One can deduce that the key contributor is centered on the leadership style and the influence the leader in an organisation can wield in relation to knowledge development in team players. Leaders influence others to perform a task by using four main characteristics of leadership, namely relationship development, receiving and disseminating information, influencing individuals and decision formulation ability. To do this in an inspiring manner that shares knowledge is beneficial for all and is truly transformational in nature.

By reviewing the leadership styles in the business sector, to ascertain the level of knowledge that is being imparted, shared or transferred through coaching and mentoring leadership traits to middle managers and whether leaders in industry are builders of empowered teams or destructors of teams. Further to this whether the leadership style is conducive to sharing or effecting knowledge transfer. Often the hierarchical structure has multiple layers in place, not only between the lowest level and highest level, but amongst management themselves.

THE PROBLEM

The Ideal situation is the free flow of knowledge between management that creates a team of specialists in their various disciplines that readily share knowledge and create an environment that allows for decision making that does not require a micro-management style but rather enables the developmental growth of individuals to take place. The essence of which determines the method of which this transference takes place and by the use of which medium since various methods of transference of knowledge exist, whether e-learning, self-learning, coaching and or mentoring.

The problem faced by these private businesses are that they are often owned by private shareholders whom have no relevant experience and run by General Managers who are micro managed from the same shareholders. The result of which the General Manager will make all the decisions and micro manage the reporting line managers. The extent of this is that neither transformation nor capacity building can take place, no real transfer of skills or knowledge happens. The line managers become disillusioned and are either dismissed or leave, some from the industry entirely. This does not support Employment Equity, neither does it support Broad Based Black Economic Empowerment, which both support the principle of transformation albeit to fulfil previous racial inequalities as a cornerstone to the development of economic progression.

This book explores whether leadership is either enabling or disabling in nature has an effect on the attrition rate of line managers in the business sector of the economy, further to this whether the lost line managers stay in the industry or move to other sectors within the economy. This book will further formulate a framework to enable transformation and enrich the value of creating a knowledge vault within a business unit.

Direct benefit to the industry is that although private businesses are by nature relatively small, the business unit can operate with similar expertise as large corporate units if the sharing of knowledge amongst the management is encouraged. Attrition will always take place, this however does not need to be due to poor empowerment of line managers that become despondent and seek other economic endeavors. The cost benefit of which are a saving in recruitment and the saving of re-training a new member of staff. Should this not happen, private industries in South Africa will receive additional pressure to conform to ever changing Broad Based Black Economic Empowerment pressures to adapt business strategies along the lines of transformation and ultimately will undergo economic hardship. This is largely due to the fact that transformation is not carried out in the true sense but rather in a numeric sense.

Balance between shareholder responsibility, exceeding of customer expectations and managing an effective workforce requires a prioritization of goals and objectives; however, should the balance not be maintained disequilibrium will occur at the expense of the other cornerstones. The essence of which hinges on the ability of the transference of knowledge amongst management to be focused on maximizing value whilst maintaining equilibrium. By not sharing in the knowledge and transferring of skills the talent pool within the organisation will dwindle until such a time that the organisation cannot operate as a functioning unit. The value contribution of the business unit to all stakeholders becomes inefficient.

Dr Peter Gregersen © 2024

Transference of knowledge in an organisation is fundamental to the success of any organisation. This is further supported by the relevance of best practice transfer of knowledge and skills in the Cuban tourism sector as a key to the growth and development of this sector.

To design a framework for this is to understand the fundamental responsibilities of running an organisation in order to add value, not only financial returns but also value to staff and customers. The sharing of skills and knowledge is paramount to valued transformation that enriches all who embrace it and enriches the values of all stakeholders creating a competitive advantage. The essence of which is to create a framework for leadership transference of knowledge.

KNOWLEDGE TRANSFER AND LEADERSHIP

By exploring the existence of knowledge transfer as a key link to leadership traits and to explore the mechanisms of knowledge transfer with the ability to increase retention within any sector. The context of this within the environment is that it is of a multi-disciplinary environment encouraging concomitant skills. These skills need to exist to ensure consumer satisfaction and need to be driven by the relevant team players. This can only happen if the relevant knowledge and decision-making processes are in place for effective problem solving to be achieved and are supported by leadership. Mechanisms for the transfer of knowledge exist in two paradigms, explicit and implicit. The obvious explicit are known through policies and procedures as an example. The implicit mechanisms are of a more complex nature and rely on the cognitive ability of the participants in problem solving. This requires mentorship, guidance and discussions to take place for the implicit knowledge to be transferred. However, the linkages between knowledge management and transformational leadership where the management of knowledge is not the control derived from management practices but the sharing of knowledge in a community of participants by leaders has a greater probability within the transformational leadership trait than other traits. This chapter explores the roles of leaders and in particular the empowering leader to the transformational leader. In addition, this chapter looks at the mechanisms of knowledge transfer and the roles that this leadership style has on retention of staff.

Transfer of knowledge within the any sector is generally conducted via the experiential training method and direct mentorship and group problem solving techniques in order to ensure consistent reliable solutions to problems.

LEADERSHIP

Leaders influence others to perform a task by using four main characteristics of leadership, namely relationship development, receiving and disseminating information, influencing individuals and decision formulation ability. This is broken down further in choosing three critical elements of transformational leadership styles.

1. Captivating and inspiring Leadership.
2. Cerebral Incitement.
3. Individual attention.

This is further explained in the role of these three sub headings as follows:

Captivating and inspiring Leadership highlights the need for the leader to motivate and inspire people around them, sharing organisational visions, creating a road map to success and to whom subordinates naturally look up to.

Cerebral Incitement is characterized by the mental limitations that have been stretched by the leader whom encourages knowledge sharing and innovative responses to challenges that often require new perspectives and ideas to solve.

Individual attention characteristics are that individual's needs, aspirations, beliefs and interaction are attended to by the leader in order for individual development and progression to take place.

Leadership undeniably plays an important role in the transference of knowledge, in that non-autocratic leaders share and disseminate knowledge that flows amongst team members and as such empowers the team in such a way that the knowledge base of the team improves. The significance of this finding is that the skill base of all members in the team improves and is an enabling transaction that is seen as transforming for the improvement of all parties. The creation of knowledge reservoirs and the flow of knowledge in organisations starts with the individual participants of the organisation, followed by procedures, structures, culture and embedded systems of operations.

Dr Peter Gregersen © 2024

The knowledge attained and gleaned from members is shared amongst participants both directly through training and development and formal structures of information dissemination as well is indirectly through implicit methods such as observation and leadership walking the talk, setting an example and sharing decision making processes. This sharing of knowledge through mentoring, experiential learning and on job training is in essence knowledge management that confirms that a large part of an organisations knowledge is held by individuals and as such the transference amongst senior managers benefits the organisation as a whole.

Dr Peter Gregersen © 2024

The importance of knowledge of team members that share their field of expertise and by working cohesively, the performance of the organisation improves as all team members improve when the acquisition of knowledge increases. This though is dependent on the individual's cognitive and cerebral ability to absorb the transference of knowledge.

Tacit knowledge of individuals is an important resource for an organisation and as such the management of this knowledge should be focused on disseminating the knowledge for the benefit of the entire organisation by making this knowledge more readily available to all participants.

Dr Peter Gregersen © 2024

MECHANISMS OF KNOWLEDGE TRANSFER

Research has shown that a model of knowledge transfer does take place for solution findings of problems, further to this shows that prior knowledge and experience will use a cognitive framework in solving problems. The following model is significant.

Stages of the transfer process for novice problem solving

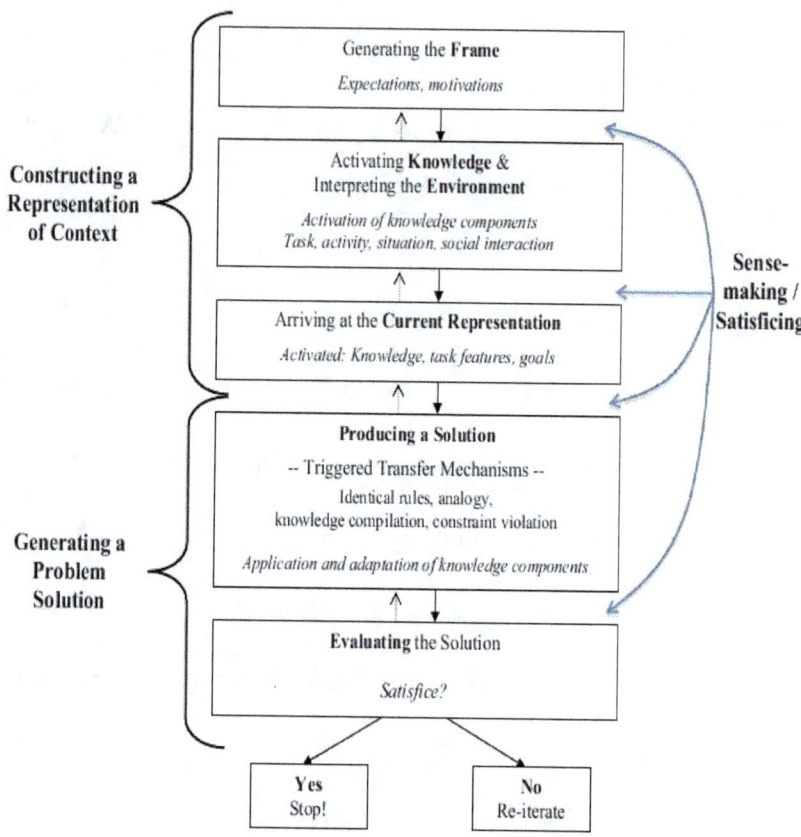

FIGURE 1   Stages of the transfer process for novices solving a problem (color figure available online).

(Source: Nokes-Malach and Mestre, 2013)

This tacit knowledge in reality is difficult to transfer as it is embedded in the individual's memory and as such requires deep interactions between participants in a team to facilitate the transfer of this embedded knowledge, where conversely the explicit knowledge is often codified and are able to be transferred easily in the form of procedures and policies or even as rules and codes of conduct. This is further supported by the social interactions within a group as additionally important to the mechanism by which knowledge is transferred in a tacit manner.

The savings to an organisation and the benefits to an organisation that encourages the tacit transfer of knowledge are significant. The role then is for the organisation to encourage this transfer of knowledge through effective leadership practices.

By virtue of this, the role of leadership that is not only to be driven and passionate but focusing on achieving organisational success through the commitment of the rest of the team in a proactive energetic approach leads the leader to become an effective leader. This commitment of the followers to the leader is most effective in a socialized power motive that strives to achieve organisational goals and vision and leads to organisational long term success. Effective leaders that are empowering that facilitate knowledge transference are more successful, hence the move to a more transformational leadership style is preferred. This is further supported by the role that transformational leaders take in not only ensuring the survival of the organisation but the supportive leadership style of encouraging team members through empowering them in decision making.

KNOWLEDGE TRANSFER

Research confirms the need for modern organisations to use transference of knowledge as a key component in the organisations arsenal for survival and is gaining significant support from corporate leadership. Common use of experiential training, mentoring, coaching and community of practice tied in with the value of one on one discussions abound as the key methods used to illicit the transfer of knowledge. Further to this the importance of a reciprocal trust relationship between the participants to allow this cognitive tacit knowledge transfer to take place is important.

METHODS OF TRANSFERENCE

The experiential training that is undertaken in industries is possibly the most frequently used method of training that is undertaken, this however focuses predominantly on the practical side of the operation, how to complete a particular task and does not necessarily delve into the problem-solving solution finding sphere.

Mentoring and coaching allows for the individuals intelligence and cognitive behavior to be engaged in order for the development from a transformational context to take place. This is evident in the process of mentoring being;

1. Experience - bringing real knowledge into the discussion and allowing the mentor to gain insight into the problem solving process.
2. Reflection- allowing for the understanding of and realisation on

what has taken place and how the situation should be handled.
3. Conclusion- allowing for the mentor to draw conclusions that are now obvious as the correct solution.
4. Experiment- allowing the mentor to practice finding the correct solutions thereby making a community of practice apparent for the participants.

The acceptance of all the transference of knowledge and knowledge sharing desire of the organisation hinges on the ability of the leader to embrace the need for this to take place.

Typically, in the business environment the organisation is operated under three pillars namely Shareholder responsibility, Human Resource responsibility and Customer responsibility.

Dr Peter Gregersen © 2024

Typical business responsibility model

Typical business responsibility model

Shareholder responsibility

employee responsibility	Customer responsibility

Dr Peter Gregersen © 2024

The short comings of this are that the leadership transfer of knowledge is not optimized and merely focuses on attaining and equilibrium between the pillars, the following diagram is the preferred framework.

Divergent Leadership Knowledge Vault model

Dr Peter Gregersen © 2024

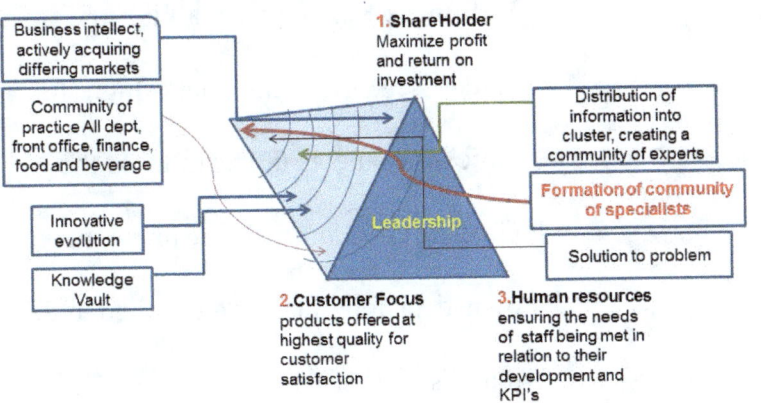

P Gregersen

EMPOWERING LEADERSHIP

The empowering leader effectively has eight qualities or behaviors that enhance

Dr Peter Gregersen © 2024

individual growth and similarly on building individuals' capabilities.

Leading by example, walking the talk, the leader sets the benchmark high for work ethic and expects the team to do the same.

Coaching, guiding the team to make their own decisions and as such better decision makers.

Encouragement, the leader recognizes inputs from the team members and with positive affirmation pushes the team forward.

Participative decision making, the leader encourages all team members to get involved and share insights into solving problems.

Dr Peter Gregersen © 2024

Informing, the ability of the leader to share information and guidance on how business decision making has been made and the reasons pertaining to these decisions.

Showing concern, the ability of the leader to have genuine empathy for the team members and the ability to ensure the well-being of these members.

Team interaction, the ability of the leader to be present and available for the team.

Group management, the ability of the leader to effectively manage the team and strive for participants to self- manage and self – evaluate.

This then moves the leader from an enabling leader through the empowering phase of leadership to that of a transformational leader.

Development of transformational leadership

The origins of the theory of transformational leadership stems from James MacGregor Burns' theory in 1978. This pivotal work opened a superfluous number of investigations into this area of leadership that has resulted in a clearer understanding of what transformational leadership entails. By agreeing with Burns one can identify two types of leaders, namely transactional and transformational and it is further accentuated that these leaders are poles apart, a dichotomous relationship in essence. This led to the conclusion that found that enablers and disablers' wherein the difference of managers and leaders is explored that uplift followers to achieve or erode followers resulting in failure of the organisation. The essence of this is that organisations have embryonic intelligence within itself and leaders who use this dormant intelligence achieve better results than leaders who assume that they themselves are the knowledge bank of the organisation. The multiplier will access the intelligence from the team to solve problems and create winning solutions by engaging with team players and conversely the diminishers will focus on reducing expenses and increasing revenues. This does not harvest the embryonic intelligence from the participants and does not build a platform of knowledge transfer or lend itself to a proactive transformational leadership quality.

The basis of Burns theory is that the two types, transactional leads to effort and rewards akin to trading of give and take in its simplest form and transformational that paradoxically changes and uplifts followers and leaders. The basis of Burns' theory is premised on Maslow's theory that people want to attain betterment and some strive to realize the level of self- actualization.

Emphasizes should be the need for leaders to recognize and interact with followers in a manner that develops and mentors' followers with behavior that is inclusive and non- dismissive which will result in organisational success. This notion is consistent with Burn's theory that transformational leadership is the ability to inspire and motivate followers to greater achievement that results in greater achievement for the leader.

The link leadership plays in inspiring, developing and intellectually growing people whilst sharing of knowledge between both the follower and the leader is a key factor.

The demand for modern leaders to be transformational in motivating and inspiring followers is now seen as the preferred leader due to the requirements of human resources in ensuring personal wellness and personal job satisfaction. This ensures communication from leaders to be on point with addressing individual needs, motivating, inspiring, encouraging meaningful two- way communication and setting of values and guidelines of behavior that followers want to emulate.

Transformation can be described as a change from one state to another within an organisation. The change occurs in both the individual and the organisation in such a manner that it cannot be undone. This is further explained that the individual needs to be engaged in the process and desires for this transformation to take place with the mental cognitive value of transformation being understood as being fundamental to the knowledge transfer that gives rise to an increased value system.

The following nine principles for transformation which are the foundation upon which transformation takes place and as such if in place ensure that transformation is successful.

1. Transformation is not an alternative expression for change.

2. Pre-requisite for agreement to change.
3. Require a second order change, radical change of individual and organisation on all levels.
4. Change cannot be reversed.
5. Change affects all aspects of individuals and organisational life.
6. This change requires the release of control.
7. This change requires an aspect of risk, including fear and or loss.
8. Always involves the broadening of outlook on where one fits in society.
9. Increases the movement up one's value and belief system.

A transformational leader is an empowering leader, and as such the knowledge sharing and development of trusting relationships results in an improvement of organisational performance and an empowerment for the follower and leader. The outcome of the process is where the follower can become a leader due to the transference of knowledge and the broadening of outlooks.

Transformation model

The transformation model is comprised of four components which need to be integrated in practice in order to achieve the outcome of inspiring and supporting people in the organisation. The components of the transformational leadership model will be elaborated below.

1. The core of the transformation model is the fundamental understanding of the cognitive self. The value system, beliefs, morals and ethics based in consistent honesty and trust, the

personal qualities of the leader need to be based on sound values.
2. The leader needs to engage with individuals in an empathetic understanding genuine manner that instils belief.
3. This then leads to the engagement of the individual into the organisation that develops and builds through a culture of team work and inspiration that achieves their goals.
4. Through a shared vision all accept change and progress forward with increased knowledge.

Dr Peter Gregersen © 2024

Transformational leadership

(Source: http://decadesofchange.weebly.com/managing-change.html)

Dr Peter Gregersen © 2024

CHARACTERISTICS

The characteristics of a transformational leader are:

1. Individualised consideration, the extent to which the follower's needs are taken care of by the leader, mentoring, coaching, empathetic listening, caring, supportive, guidance and personal care.
2. Inspirational motivation, the extent to which the follower is inspired by the leader that gives a sense of purpose and the particular success of this hinges on the leader possessing visionary skills that are enunciated in an inspiring fashion that encourages the followers to identify with the visions.
3. Intellectual stimulation, the extent to which leaders encourage meaningful

input from followers that are encouraged to give innovative input and share in knowledge transfer.
4. Idealized influence, the extent to which followers wish to emulate the leader, where the leader is seen to be a role model and a compass for ethics, values, morals, behaviour, honesty, trust and leads with passion.

In addition to the characteristics stated above, transformational leaders possess charisma which is illustrative through being inspirational, the ability of the leader to charm and win over followers that encourages the followers to want to achieve the vision portrayed by the leader.

These leadership traits of a transformational leader require a leader to be forward looking and one whom gives guidance and understanding to a team, this is not in essence transformation in itself but merely the groundwork for transformation to be able to take place and is the nurturing ground for the transference of knowledge within the team.

Retention of skilled staff

As staff are seen as human capital in an organisation, the investment through training, development and nurturing of these skilled employees creates a competitive advantage and as such leads to the Human capital theory, which in essence is the investment into staff development to increase productivity. Further to this leads one to view these retention strategies in line with the resource-based view that ensures that the development of human resources is fundamental in ensuring that the development of one's staff creates a scenario that ensures the value of the organisation is enhanced and becomes hard to imitate as it is seen as rare and valuable. Added to this the human resources function of acquiring talent and retaining talent is now seen as a priority and in particular staff with high potential and skills set as this is seen as a primary source for a competitive advantage. High staff turnover rates are endemic to all industries, in particular ones which are highly labour intensive, such as customer service staff, who are able to easily migrate to other industries. To mitigate this retention strategies employed by the industry are put in place and include. Fast track promotions for talented individuals, competitive salaries and pay structures, performance bonuses, training and development and retirement benefits. Common place in South Africa are the following, share options due to the Broad Based Black Economic Empowerment initiatives, and subsidies such as housing, food, transport, entertainment allowances, medical aids and funeral benefits amongst other initiatives.

Dr Peter Gregersen © 2024

The internal and external challenges faced by organisations today require leadership that inspires and support the people within the organisation to achieve the performance targets. Leadership is the driver of ensuring that organisation become prominent within their industries.

The clarification of what transformational leadership from James MacGregor Burns' theory in 1978 provided basic principles on the evolution of the concept with the transformation model emphasizing four focus areas which provide the framework.

The characteristics of a transformational leader is made of the "4 Is" with an additional character of charisma as the key factor, Moreover, a transformational leader provides guidance to the team and this necessitates the leader to be forward looking.

The impact of transference of knowledge by leadership on the performance of the organisation results in an increase of the level of motivation and performance beyond the expectation by the members of the organisation. In addition to the performance levels, the members of staff have gained knowledge thus improving performance. This when tied into the tacit and explicit transfer of knowledge and the importance of retention strategies that give an organisation a competitive advantage leads one to the importance of leadership in guiding the process.

to include the leadership framework that supports the paradigms in the context of the creation of a community of experts that support the transfer of knowledge.

Dr Peter Gregersen © 2024

Leadership correlation with typical responsibility model

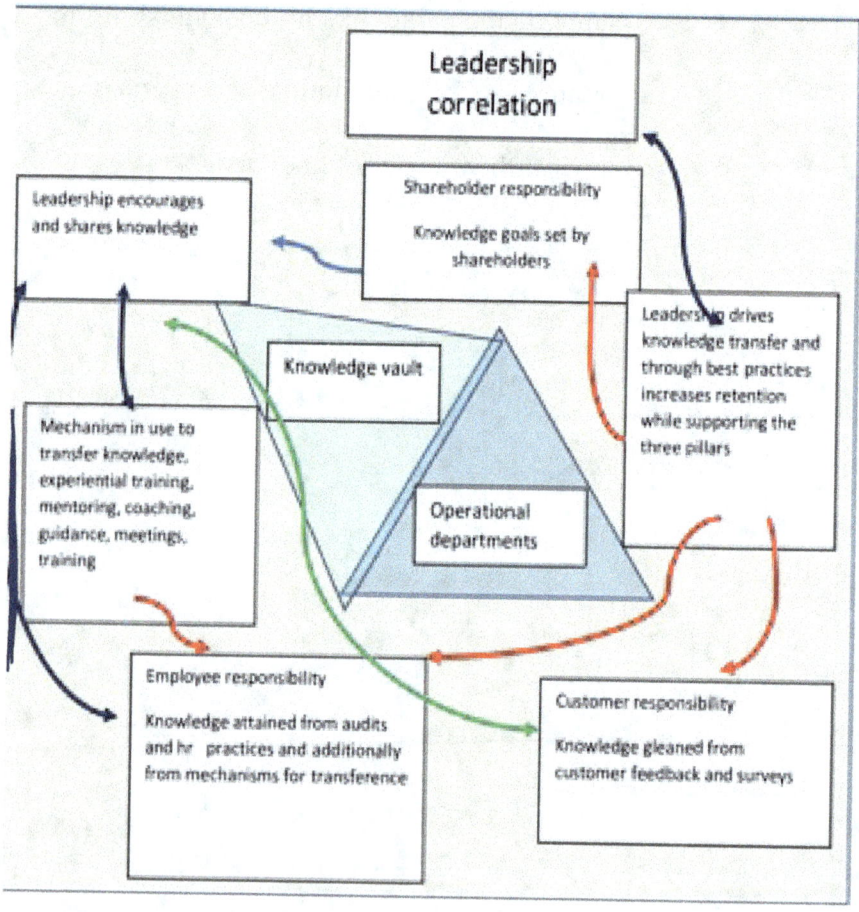

Dr Peter Gregersen © 2024

The significance of this is that it leads to the construction of a Divergent Leadership Knowledge Vault model.

Divergent Leadership Knowledge Vault model

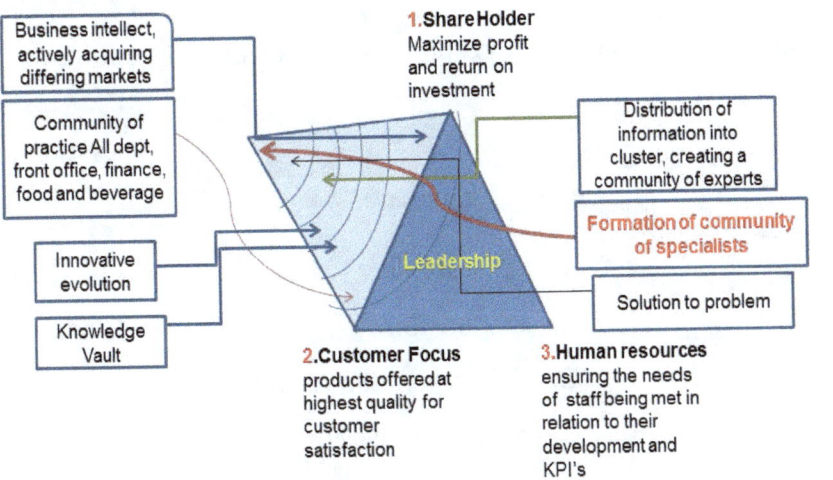

P Gregersen

The basis of decision making is cognitive in its self and more specifically in a significant cerebral

Dr Peter Gregersen © 2024

manner in making judgments with reasoning, logic and memory. In addition, aided through a community of practice guided through both explicit and implicit knowledge attainment through the transference of knowledge that support the three paradigms of an organisation the cognitive response that is desired is achieved.

The three pillars are:

1. Shareholder / owner / director responsibility.
2. Customer responsibility.
3. Staff responsibility.

This is a fundamental way in leading as this ensures a balanced approach in making decisions and leading a workforce to achieve maximum results away from a straight linear approach. By approaching this in a community of practice way, the practitioner becomes an expert, then a specialist in the required field with the use of innovation dependable on intelligence quotient (I.Q), emotional intelligence(E.Q), and only if the intellectual approach and ability is present that aids in the transference of knowledge to create a knowledge vault, this sharing of decision making principles and advice amongst participants improves all of the receiving individuals cognitive abilities regardless of educational background.

The shareholder responsibility pillar is ensuring that in all decisions that are made and, in any guidance, or direction given to the workforce being executive management or line workers the fiduciary responsibility of the company is adhered to often through explicit knowledge guided by policies and procedures. Further to this all controls and systems and all return on investment (ROI) decisions are made. Co-ordination, common purpose, delegation, decision making, planning, production, forecasting, controls, finance and quality are also key elements that are managed under the banner of Shareholder responsibility. The direction of the company is set into motion and puzzling questions are answered and resolutions are found in the contrasts of opinions.

Dr Peter Gregersen © 2024

The second pillar being customer responsibility is a leadership style that is often ignored, however without customers the business would fold this is intrinsic and the goal is not to meet customer expectations but to exceed in them. In making of the first decisions for shareholders and to balance it to one side would be to ensure customer satisfaction, this leadership style require one to balance needs of the shareholders to that of the customers' needs, with the customer receiving the best possible product at the highest quality at the most profitable for the company. Leadership shows an increase in public awareness, civil responsibilities, marketing and of gaining a competitive advantage.

Dr Peter Gregersen © 2024

The third pillar is the Staff responsibility. True leadership takes care of the human resources component of the business. Parameters are set to operate within and allow the staff to operate within those parameters and autonomous control is given to managers allowing for real immediate solutions to problems. This leadership style that balances human resources with customers and shareholder responsibilities through the creation of a knowledge vault that strives to create a community of specialists from a community of practice where decisions and thought processes are shared allows for the development of each individual to draw on the expertise of all individual persons.

Dr Peter Gregersen © 2024

The three corners are held with concomitance in that if one corner receives too much emphasis the pyramid will collapse, as the realization of reliability on one corner is not sufficient to support all corners but rather a shared quality significant association is needed in building a community of specialists rather than mere participants.

In order to attain the success of the business, the business needs to ensure it has 1, Ability 2, to consistently 3, meet the customers expectations. This ability talks to the competence of the employees, which implies the need for knowledge. The consistency talks to the reliability of the employees where the continuous performance is at an acceptable level that ensures that the customer receives an acceptable outcome. All of which is dependent on the access to the transference of knowledge.

CONCLUSION

Undeniably the transfer of knowledge exists, the purpose of this work was to develop a framework of leadership knowledge transfer that improves the retention rate and empowers middle management to be knowledgeable decision makers in the private business sector. This was guided by my research undertaken in analyzing the extent to which change and growth had been embraced in line with development as well as the likelihood of attrition of middle management or retention practices in place as well as the extent to which leaders transfer knowledge and by which method to middle managers.

Dr Peter Gregersen © 2024

The linkages between knowledge management and transformational leadership explored the sharing of knowledge in a community of participants. The roles of leadership in an organisational context was explored in line with transformational leadership as supported by literature. In addition, the mechanisms of knowledge transfer and the roles that leadership style and traits has on retention of staff was investigated.

The findings are that a relationship between knowledge transfer and retention strategies does indeed exist as well as between knowledge transfer and company leadership strategies of staff. However, the probability of there being a relationship between knowledge transfer and individual learning strategies cannot be supported. The reservoir of knowledge both tacit and explicit exists and through leadership and guidance allows for the development of a knowledge vault and the formation of a community of experts as described and depicted in figure above.

"Share your knowledge. It is a way to achieve immortality."
~Dalai Lama

THE END

Dr Peter Gregersen © 2024

www.ingramcontent.com/pod-product-compliance
Lightning Source LLC
Chambersburg PA
CBHW072017230526
45479CB00008B/251